Science@School | Book 3C

Properties of materials

A brief history

TODAY... 1975 The plastic PET is invented and used for bottles in place of glass... 1930 Three important plastics are invented – polystyrene, PVC and melamine... 1909 Leo Baekeland invents Bakelite... 1884 Louis Bernigaud makes an artificial fibre. It is called rayon. Also Carl Zeiss develops a glass that will not crack with heat... 1862 Alexander Parkes invents the first plastic... 1823 Charles Macintosh invents waterproof fabric: a coat made with it is called the Mackintosh... 1742 Benjamin Huntsman makes fine spring steel... 1709 Abraham Darby makes iron using coke as a fuel. This brings about the Industrial Revolution... 1493 Christopher Columbus arrives in America and brings rubber back to Europe... 200BC Concrete is invented by the Romans... 450BC Marble is used to face Greek temples... 1500BC Iron is removed from rock by heating in a very hot fire. The Iron Age begins... 3000BC The first bronze is made in Turkey by melting tin and copper together in a fire. The Bronze Age begins... 5000BC The first clay pots are fired, making them hard and watertight and able to hold liquids... 6000BC The first woven cloth is made. The first baskets are made... 8000BC Copper is used... 10,000BC The first sun-dried bricks are made... 2.4 million BC The first stone tools are made in Africa. The Stone Age begins...

For more information visit www.science-at-school.com

Dr Brian Knapp

Word list

These are some science words that you should look out for as you go through the book. They are shown using CAPITAL letters.

ABSORBENT
A material that soaks up water.

ARTIFICIAL
Something made by people and which does not occur in nature.

BEND
To turn something from being straight into a curve.

BRITTLE
Something that breaks suddenly and easily.

CONDUCTOR
A material that will let heat or electricity flow through it easily. Metals are conductors.

CRUSH
To squeeze or press until the material loses its shape.

ELASTIC
A flexible material that can be stretched, but will go back to its original shape when released.

FLEXIBLE
Something that will bend or stretch easily without breaking.

HARD
Something that will not scratch easily. Most hard materials are brittle.

INSULATOR
A material that will not let heat or electricity flow through it easily. Plastics are insulators.

MATERIAL
Anything used to make things. Plastic, wood, metal and glass, for example, are all materials.

PROPERTY
A special quality of a material – such as its strength, hardness or flexibility.

RUST
Reddish-brown coloured pitting and flaking of the surface of iron and steel.

SHATTER
To break up into many small pieces.

SOFT
Something easy to scratch.

STRETCH
To pull a material until it becomes longer.

STRONG
Something that will not break easily.

TEAR
To pull a material apart by force.

TRANSPARENT
A material that you can see through.

WATERPROOF
A material that will not soak up water.

WEAK
Something that will break easily.

Weblink: www.science-at-school.com

Contents

	Page
Word list	2
Unit 1: Materials through the ages	4
Unit 2: Hard and soft materials	6
Unit 3: Strong materials	8
Unit 4: Springy materials	10
Unit 5: Materials that bend and stretch	12
Unit 6: Brittle materials	14
Unit 7: Keeping in the heat	16
Unit 8: Soaking up water	18
Unit 9: Using metals	20
Unit 10: Using plastics	22
Index	24

Weblink: www.science-at-school.com

Materials through the ages

The more materials you have to use, the more things you can make. This is why new materials have been invented down the ages.

Anything you use to make things is called a **MATERIAL**.

Using natural materials

The first people (sometimes called Stone Age people) used only the natural materials that they found around them – materials like stone, clay, wood, animal skins and bones.

But even with these simple materials, they could make many useful and sometimes beautiful things such as axes and ploughs, arrows and bows, clothes, pots and bowls (Pictures 1 and 2).

Using metals

About 3,000 years ago, people discovered how to get new materials from rock. These were metals.

As a result, they suddenly had many new materials to work with.

At first people used metals which were soft and easy to shape – gold, silver and copper. Later they learned how to use iron, steel and many other metals.

Each new metal gave them the chance to make many new things (Picture 3). Today, metals are used to build everything from railway lines to spaceships and rockets.

Inventing plastics

Most recently of all, scientists have discovered they could make lots of materials that had never existed in the world before. These materials are made from oil and called plastics. They could be shaped into all kinds of new things.

A wooden stick is used as a handle.

A flint axe is chipped to give a sharp edge.

Gut from an animal is used as string to tie the axe head to the stick.

▼ **(Picture 2) This is a home made by bending sticks to make a frame, then covering the frame with tree bark. The bark is held down with more sticks.**

▲ **(Picture 1) Stone Age tools used only simple, natural materials. This is an axe with a handle. It uses three natural materials. It is easier to use than a hand axe.**

Weblink: www.science-at-school.com

More and more choices

As you can see, down the ages people have used more and more types of materials (Picture 4).

So what makes people choose one type of material instead of another type? This is what you will discover as you read the rest of this book.

▲ (Picture 3) By the Victorian Age, people were using many kinds of metal, but there were no plastics. As a result, what they sold in their shops looked very different from what we see in shops today. The objects in the shop front are baths made of a material called galvanised iron.

Summary
- You make things with materials.
- A material can be natural or man-made.
- Each material has its own range of uses.
- Each time we invent a new material we make our world a more varied place.

▼ (Picture 4) These astronauts make use of thousands of materials, some invented in the last few years specially for use in space.

5

Hard and soft materials

Every material is different. We call these differences PROPERTIES. Hardness is one important property of materials.

Why are some materials **HARD** and others **SOFT**? It all depends on what they are made of (Picture 1).

One way to think about a material is to imagine it as being made up of tiny blocks of material all held together by glue. If the blocks are hard and the glue is tough, the whole material is hard, but if the blocks or the glue are weak, then the material is soft*.

A rub and scratch test

A very soft material will rub away using just your finger (Pictures 2 and 4). But not many materials are as soft as this. Those that are a bit harder can be scratched with a fingernail.

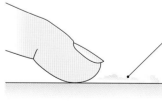

A very soft material, such as soil, can be broken up by rubbing.

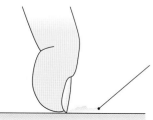

A soft material, such as chalk, can be scratched, but not rubbed away.

▲ (Picture 1) The world's hardest natural material is a diamond. You can't cut a diamond. All you can do is split it into smaller pieces.

◄ (Picture 2) If a material is very soft, it will easily be rubbed away. An eraser, or rubber, is used in just this way. It is softer than paper, so it won't harm the paper and yet it is harder than the mark made by a pencil. So the eraser rubs the pencil mark away, and the paper rubs the eraser away.

(*NOTE: Do not confuse soft with flexible, such as when you touch woollen cloth.)

Weblink: www.science-at-school.com

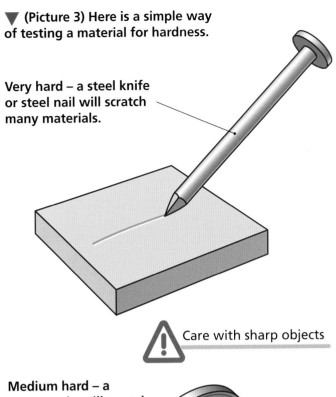

▼ (Picture 3) Here is a simple way of testing a material for hardness.

Very hard – a steel knife or steel nail will scratch many materials.

⚠ Care with sharp objects

Medium hard – a copper coin will scratch many soft materials.

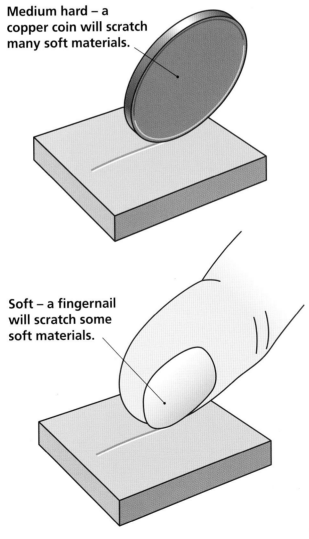

Soft – a fingernail will scratch some soft materials.

You can compare the hardness of all sorts of materials using just a steel knife or steel nail, a copper coin and your fingernail (Picture 3).

Steel is a very hard material. It will scratch the copper coin. That means the copper is softer than steel. But a fingernail can't scratch the coin, so the copper is harder than the fingernail.

Now, with just these three materials, you can test the hardness of any material you choose.

Choosing a suitable material

Why would you want to know if a material is hard or soft? Well, what if you wanted to cut something? You would want to use a hard material for the knife. It would have to be hard if it were to cut other materials.

Another use for a hard material would be as a case to protect TVs, computers and other delicate or soft materials. Hard plastic is often used for this.

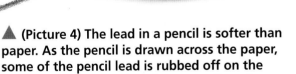

▲ (Picture 4) The lead in a pencil is softer than paper. As the pencil is drawn across the paper, some of the pencil lead is rubbed off on the surface of the paper, leaving a pencil mark.

Summary
• Materials vary in their hardness.
• We can test for hardness with simple materials.
• We usually choose the hardness to match what we want the material to do.

Weblink: www.science-at-school.com

Strong materials

A STRONG material won't BEND, TEAR, CRUSH or SHATTER easily.

It takes a lot of effort to break a strong material. All kinds of materials can be strong (Picture 1). Stone is a strong material that can be used to make tall buildings. Steel is a strong material that can be used to make motor cars.

Some, more surprising, materials are strong, too. Rubber, for example, is also a strong material, even though it moves easily. This is because, although it will STRETCH, it won't break easily.

Testing for strength

There are many ways you can find out if something is strong enough for your needs.

For example, you could place the material you want to test on two supports (Picture 2). You could then put heavy weights on it. If the material breaks when just a small weight is added, then it is WEAK. But if it will stand up to a heavy weight, then it is strong.

You can perform a similar test to see how well a material will resist bending (Picture 3).

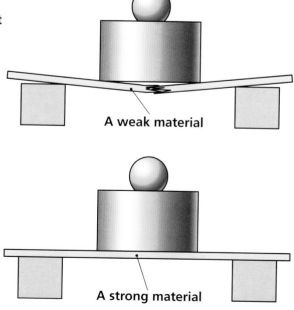

◄ (Picture 1) The Space Shuttle has to be built using very strong materials so that it can successfully fly to and from space.

▼ (Picture 2) Testing to see if a material will break.

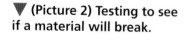

A weak material

A strong material

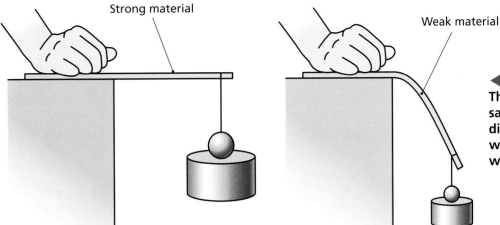

Strong material

Weak material

◀ (Picture 3) Testing for strength. This test uses two rods of the same size, but made from different materials. The same weight is hung on each rod. The weaker material bends or breaks.

Combining materials makes them stronger

Many materials can be made stronger by combining them with other materials. A bowl, for example, can be made of strips of paper and wallpaper paste. Wallpaper paste and strips of paper are both too weak to support anything. But they can be combined to make a strong bowl.

The paper is cut into strips and the strips are pasted together. In Picture 4, an inflatable ball has been used as a support for the bowl until the paste has set.

When the paper and paste have dried, the air is let out of the ball and it is removed. The dried paper and glue have now been changed into a new material – one strong enough to keep fruit and other heavy objects in.

▼ (Picture 4) Making a strong bowl out of a combination of weak materials.

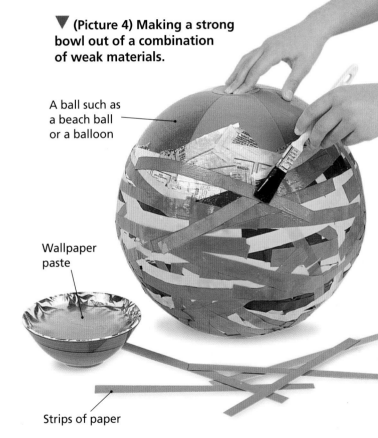

A ball such as a beach ball or a balloon

Wallpaper paste

Strips of paper

Summary
• Materials are strong if they don't break or change shape without warning.
• Weak materials can often be made stronger by combining them.

Weblink: www.science-at-school.com

Springy materials

Springy materials will change shape when you pull them or push them, but return to their original shape when you let them go.

Anything that will change shape without breaking is called a **FLEXIBLE** material. Springy materials are one kind of flexible material. This is how they work.

Materials with a memory

Springy materials all have a sort of 'memory'. They 'know' what shape they

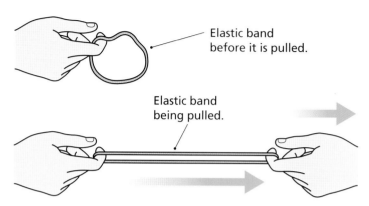

Elastic band before it is pulled.

Elastic band being pulled.

Elastic band released.

▶ **(Picture 1) This balloon will change shape when it is squeezed, but when released, it will spring back to the shape it started with.**

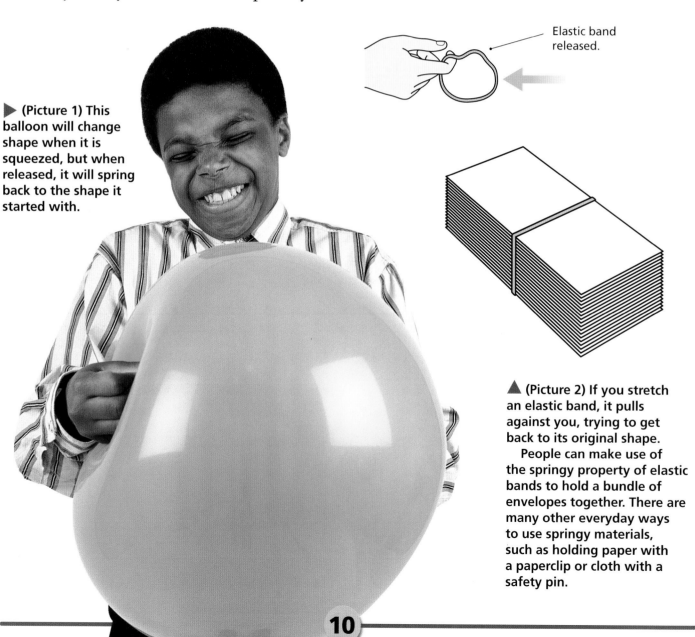

▲ **(Picture 2) If you stretch an elastic band, it pulls against you, trying to get back to its original shape.**
   People can make use of the springy property of elastic bands to hold a bundle of envelopes together. There are many other everyday ways to use springy materials, such as holding paper with a paperclip or cloth with a safety pin.

are and they don't like changing to a new shape. So when you change their shape by pulling on them, then let go, they tend to spring back into the shape they started with. We use the words springy, or **ELASTIC**, to describe this property (Picture 1).

Whatever you do, you cannot get elastic materials to take on a new shape (Picture 2).

You may be wearing elastic materials such as stretch tights and stretch socks right now. You can also find elastic materials in the rubber seals around the fridge, the cooker and the doors of cars.

Metal springs

You may not think of metal as a springy material, but when it is coiled up it can make a powerful spring (Picture 3).

Steel springs stretch less easily than rubber or plastic, so steel springs are used with heavy weights (Picture 4).

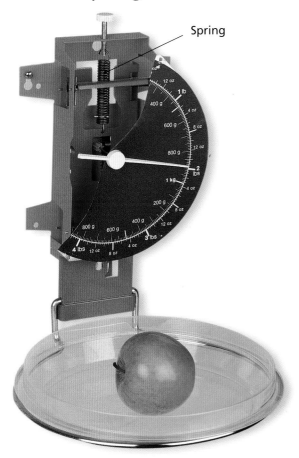

▲ (Picture 4) A scale for weighing food uses a spring. In this example, the scale has been partly cut away so that you can see the spring inside the case.

▼ (Picture 3) A coiled metal spring will stretch when a weight is hung from it. When the weight is taken away the spring goes back to its original size.

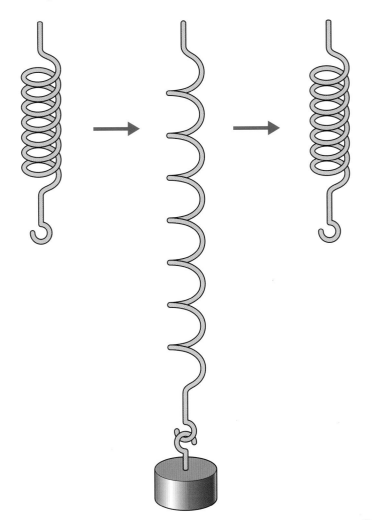

Summary
• Elastic materials can be stretched, but they always go back to the shape they started with (unless you stretch them too far).

Weblink: www.science-at-school.com

Materials that bend and stretch

Many materials can easily be pulled or bent into new shapes. They are another kind of flexible material.

Some materials can easily be made into new shapes. For example, you can bend a piece of wire into a new shape (Picture 1), or you can pull a toffee into a new shape (Picture 2). The clothes you are wearing keep changing shape as you move.

There are many flexible materials of this kind in the world. They are not springy, and they do not break easily, they simply change from one shape into another. Plasticine is another good example of a material that will bend and stretch and yet hold new shapes (Picture 3).

Thin means flexible

Thin things can be put into new shapes more easily than thick ones because there is less material to move. This is why a thin sheet of aluminium or plastic can be bent easily (Picture 4), but a thick block of aluminium or plastic is far less flexible.

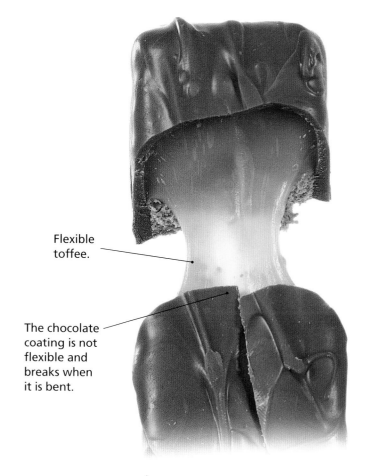

Flexible toffee.

The chocolate coating is not flexible and breaks when it is bent.

▲ **(Picture 2) The toffee in this bar of chocolate holds a new shape when it is stretched or bent.**

▼ **(Picture 1) Wire can easily be bent into a new shape, which it will hold. It can even be bent back to its original shape. Wire is flexible, so it can do all this without breaking.**

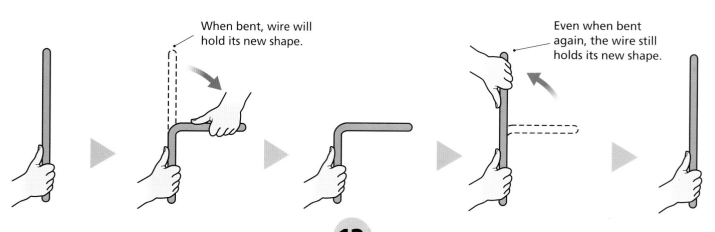

When bent, wire will hold its new shape.

Even when bent again, the wire still holds its new shape.

Weblink: www.science-at-school.com

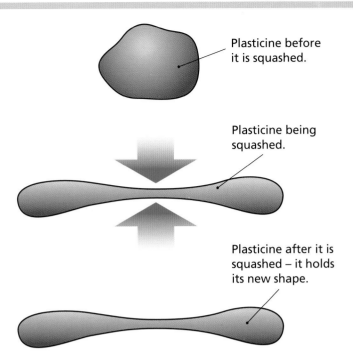

Plasticine before it is squashed.

Plasticine being squashed.

Plasticine after it is squashed – it holds its new shape.

▲ (Picture 3) When Plasticine is pinched, rolled or pulled it makes a new shape. It is flexible and will bend and stretch, but it is not springy (elastic).

Flexible fibres

One of the most easily bent shapes is a long thin rod. We call a very small rod, a fibre. Cloth is flexible because it is made from long, thin fibres (Picture 5).

Even glass can be flexible when it is made into a fibre. The cables used to carry telephone messages under our streets are made of thin, flexible glass fibres.

Many common fibres are metals. For example, the wires in an electricity cable are made of long threads of copper. This is why you can move the cable around easily.

◀ (Picture 4) This hot food container is sealed by pushing up the edge of the flexible aluminium base over the cardboard top.

▲ (Picture 5) Cloth and rope are flexible because they are made from long, thin fibres.

Summary
• Some materials can be reshaped time after time.
• Materials that are bendable are mainly shaped into rods (such as fibres) and thin sheets.
• Almost any material can be made flexible when it is a fibre – even glass.

Weblink: www.science-at-school.com

Brittle materials

Some materials break very suddenly. They are brittle.

Everyone knows that you have to be careful with some materials or they will break. Tap a china cup, or a drinking glass, too hard and it will shatter into many pieces. Chocolate is brittle too, which is why it breaks into chunks.

We use the word **BRITTLE** for a material that breaks suddenly (Picture 1).

Brittle materials are held together inside so tightly that they can't move. So when the materials are pulled, twisted or struck a blow, the 'glue' holding them together simply snaps.

Which materials are brittle?

Many brittle things are also hard. Brittle materials include glass, rock, concrete, china and even bone. If they are hit with a hammer, they may smash into tiny pieces (Picture 2).

Ice and a few plastics are also brittle (Picture 3), but very few metals or fibres are brittle.

▼ **(Picture 1) A stick of chalk is brittle. It will snap if bent.**

Stick of chalk

Sudden and unpredictable break

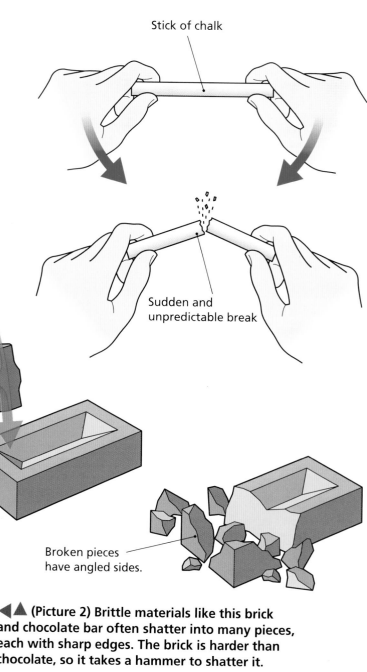

Broken pieces have angled sides.

◀◀ ▲ **(Picture 2) Brittle materials like this brick and chocolate bar often shatter into many pieces, each with sharp edges. The brick is harder than chocolate, so it takes a hammer to shatter it.**

Why are brittle things used?

You may think something that smashes easily is useless. But we use glass and china all the time. We put up with their brittleness because their other properties are so good. Glass, for example, may be brittle, but we use it because we can see through it (it is **TRANSPARENT**). Some spectacles use lenses made of glass.

Brittle materials are only weak when twisted or pulled or struck (Picture 4).

We can make brittle materials less likely to break by combining them with other materials. Builders, for example, put steel rods inside concrete (this is called reinforced concrete). Car makers sandwich sheets of plastic between glass in windscreens. This stops the windscreen from shattering during an accident.

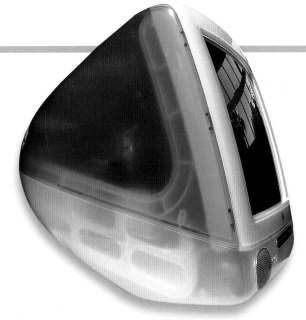

▲ (Picture 3) A computer is protected by a hard plastic case. The case is brittle and will smash when dropped or hit.

Summary
- A brittle material will snap without warning.
- Most brittle materials are hard.
- Brittle materials are usually strong.
- Brittle materials can be made tougher.

▼ (Picture 4) If a stone hits a window, the window is not able to bend, so it snaps, leaving a jagged hole.

Weblink: www.science-at-school.com

Keeping in the heat

To keep things warm, a material must stop heat being lost.

We all know how important it is to wear warm clothes in cold weather (Picture 1).

A material that holds the heat in is called an **INSULATOR**.

Testing insulators

There is no easy way to see whether a material lets heat through quickly or not. The only way is to test it.

▼▶ **(Picture 1) All of the materials used in ski clothing are thick. This is especially true of the clothes used to protect hands and feet, which suffer from the cold most of all.**

A simple test is to find out about how well the materials stop heat from flowing through them.

In Picture 2, the same amount of hot water has been poured into three coffee cups (the cups are made from thick foam). Three different thin materials have been placed on top of each of the cups (a piece of aluminium foil, a sheet of paper and a handkerchief).

After 30 seconds, each of the materials was touched carefully to see if the heat could be felt flowing through it. In a second test, a thermometer was used to measure the temperature of each material (Picture 3). This was a more accurate test than the touching test.

Finally, the materials were all doubled up in thickness and the test tried again. This showed that the thicker the material, the less heat flowed through.

Any materials that let heat through easily are not good insulators. They are good **CONDUCTORS** of heat.

Weblink: www.science-at-school.com

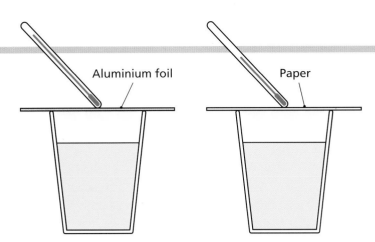

Aluminium foil

Paper

Handkerchief

◀ (Picture 2) The rate that heat can flow through a material depends on what it is made from.

Invisible insulator

There are many solid materials that won't let heat through. But there is one surprising substance that holds heat in. You can't see it, you can't touch it and you can't smell it. So what is it? It is air.

You can see lots of examples of this. Look at an insulated mug. It is made from two walls of plastic with air trapped between them (Picture 4).

▼ (Picture 3) Thickness affects how fast heat can flow through a material.

One sheet of paper.

Four sheets of paper.

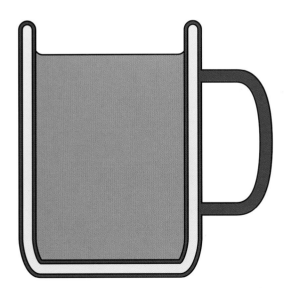

▲▶ (Picture 4) An insulated mug has a double wall of plastic to hold the liquid. Air is trapped between the walls. Plastic and air together make a good lightweight insulator.

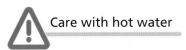 Care with hot water

Summary

• Heat flows more quickly through metals than through any other material.
• Insulators can be solid or they can make use of trapped air.

Soaking up water

Some materials keep water out. They are waterproof. Other materials soak up water. They are absorbent.

Why do some materials let water through, some soak it up and others keep it out?

Waterproof

Water is liquid. It will flow into small holes easily.

Let's start with a material that has no holes in it – a sheet of plastic (Picture 1). If you pour some water onto a plastic sheet it will all stay on the surface. Plastic is a **WATERPROOF** material.

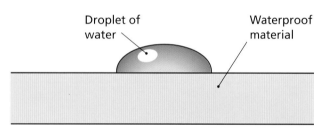

Droplet of water

Waterproof material

▲ (Picture 1) Water stays on the surface of a plastic sheet because the plastic has no holes in it. Plastic is waterproof.

▶ (Picture 2) Cotton shirts are nice and warm, but they are also absorbent and soak up water if you get caught out in the rain!

▼ (Picture 3) Water runs into the holes in-between the fibres in absorbent materials. The speed at which water does this tells you how absorbent the material is. Kitchen towels, blotting paper and sponges all soak up water. They have holes that allow water to flow into them and be held there.

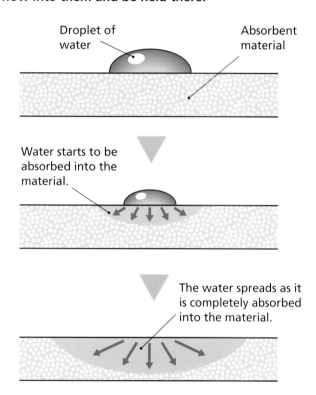

Droplet of water

Absorbent material

Water starts to be absorbed into the material.

The water spreads as it is completely absorbed into the material.

Absorbent

Absorbent means to soak up. Anything that soaks up water easily is **ABSORBENT** (Pictures 2 and 3). Water will even run upwards into an absorbent material.

If you dip the bottom of a kitchen towel into a dish of coloured water, you will see the water flow upwards. This is because the surface of the towel is covered in tiny holes. They are designed to let water in.

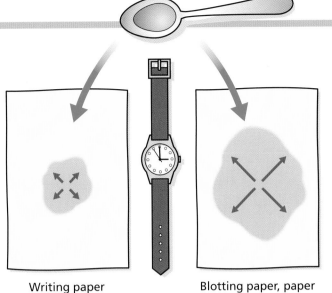

Writing paper

Blotting paper, paper towel or toilet paper

▲ **(Picture 4) This is how to compare the absorbency of different papers. Make sure they are all the same size and thickness, pour exactly the same amount of water onto each paper, then leave them for the same amount of time before checking to see how much of each paper is wet.**

Compare papers

A piece of toilet tissue soaks up a lot of water. However, a piece of writing paper soaks up much less water. This is because the holes in the writing paper are very small, so it's much harder for it to absorb water (Picture 4).

Making a water-resisting material

Water hates wax, fat, grease and oil. You can use this property to make a material water-resistant.

A thin piece of cloth would normally let water through. But if furniture polish is sprayed onto the cloth it will become almost waterproof (Picture 5). The furniture polish is a kind of wax.

Water-resistant materials are used to make outdoor clothing and umbrellas (Picture 6).

▶ **(Picture 5) Spraying furniture polish on a cloth will make the cloth almost waterproof.**

▲ **(Picture 6) Water just runs off, or sits on the surface, of water-resistant materials.**

Summary
- **Waterproof materials have no holes in them.**
- **Absorbent materials have small holes that will allow water to be held inside.**
- **Water-resistant materials are coated in wax or a similar water-hating material.**

Weblink: www.science-at-school.com

Using metals

Weight for weight, metals are among the strongest materials. They can be made into many shapes, they will stand up to high temperatures and many of them are cheap to make.

If you want a material to build a bridge or an aeroplane, you turn to metal. If you want a spring, a key or a tap – metal is the best material. And if you want something to carry electricity, then you must use a metal.

▼ (Picture 1) Motor vehicles – like this sand buggy – are all made from metal. The frame is strong steel and the engine, which gets very hot, is made with steel and aluminium. The shiny parts are a metal called chromium.

Steel

Steel is the most commonly used metal because it is so strong. It can also be rolled into sheets or pressed into shapes, like motor vehicles, because it will bend and stretch (Picture 1). Steel can be made into girders and tubes, and used to make the strong frames for skyscrapers and bridges.

But steel will not last well in damp air and it will begin to go pitted and flaky. This is called **RUST** (Picture 2).

◀ (Picture 2) A rusty steel bolt. Notice how the surface is brown and flaky.

20

Steel can be painted or coated with plastic to stop it from rusting. Steel can also be mixed with other metals to make it harder and stop it rusting. This is called stainless steel.

Aluminium

Aluminium is light and does not rust, so it is used where these properties are important – for example to make the bodies of aircraft and to make food and drink cans (Picture 3). Aluminium will bend and stretch more easily than steel.

Copper, silver and gold

Copper, silver and gold are soft metals. But they don't rust and electricity flows through them extremely well.

Copper, silver and gold have been used to make coins and jewellery for thousands of years (Picture 4).

Electricity flows easily through copper, which is why it is used in electrical wires (Picture 5).

▲ (Picture 4) This is a gold coin. Both gold and silver are scarce metals and so are valuable. Gold and silver are also soft and so can easily be stamped or bent into shapes such as jewellery.

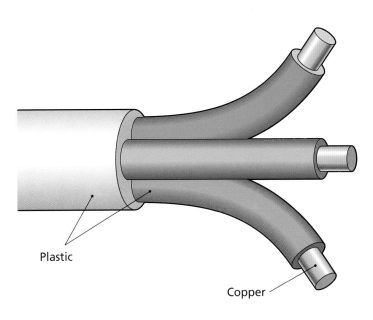

Plastic

Copper

▲ (Picture 5) Copper is a very good conductor of electricity and so is used in wires (the covering is plastic, see page 23).

▲ (Picture 3) Aluminium is widely used for cans because it will not rust and is lightweight.

Summary

• Some metals are very strong.
• Steel is the cheapest metal but it can rust.
• Aluminium is expensive, but light, and won't rust.
• Some metals are scarce and used sparingly.

Weblink: www.science-at-school.com

Using plastics

Plastics are 'designer' materials. They are all ARTIFICIAL and have millions of uses.

The first plastic was made by Alexander Parkes, in Birmingham, in 1862. It looked like tortoiseshell (Picture 1). But soon so many new plastics were invented that plastic was given the title of 'the material of a thousand uses'.

Plastics are now used everywhere (Pictures 2 and 3). For example, Terylene® is used to make the thread for clothes; Lycra® is used to make stretchable sportswear; Teflon® is used to make the surfaces of non-stick saucepans; and polythene is used for the lunch boxes you take to school.

These, and thousands of other plastics, are quite different from anything else in the world because they are all artificial.

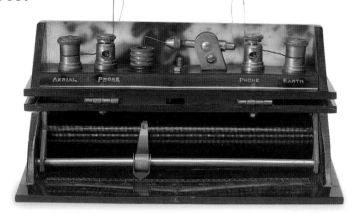

▲ (Picture 1) This very early radio used a case made of one of the first kinds of plastic. Notice the tortoiseshell look.

▼ (Picture 3) Plastics can easily be moulded. This is one reason they are used for toys like this fire engine. Look at how sharp the detail is.

▼ (Picture 2) The squeegee is made from several plastics. The handle is hard, shiny plastic, the blade is soft, elastic plastic and the back is an absorbent plastic sponge.

Weblink: www.science-at-school.com

Plastics and heat

Plastics will not let heat pass through them easily. This is why you can use plastic to keep things warm.

However, many plastics melt easily (Picture 4). Also, when some plastics burn they give off poisonous fumes.

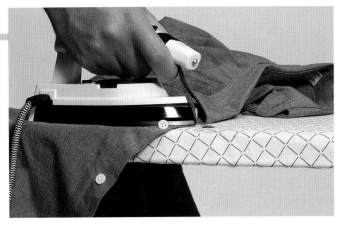

▲ (Picture 4) Because plastics melt easily, you must iron clothing made from artificial materials, like Lycra® and polyester, with a cool iron.

Plastics and electricity

One of the most important uses of plastics is to protect us from electricity. No electricity passes through plastics, so they can be used for cables and cases, and for plugs and sockets.

Plastics are light and strong

Many plastics are light, very strong and waterproof. They can also be made transparent (Picture 5). This makes plastic ideal for things like packaging food, and even computers (Picture 3, page 15).

▼ (Picture 5) Plastics can be made transparent, watertight, airtight, strong and flexible. They can be used for bottles and food bags.

Summary
- Plastics melt easily.
- Plastics are light and strong.
- Plastics are good insulators.

Weblink: www.science-at-school.com

Index

Absorbent 2, 18, 22
Artificial 2, 22-23
Bend 2, 8, 12, 20
Brittle 2, 14-15
Conductor 2, 16, 21
Crush 2, 8
Elastic 2, 10-11
Electricity 21, 23
Fibre 13, 14, 18
Flexible 2, 10-11, 12-13
Glass 14, 15
Hard 2, 6-7, 14
Insulator 2, 16-17, 23
Material 2, 4, 8-9, 10-11, 12-13, 14-15, 16-17, 18-19, 20, 22-23

Metal 4, 11, 14, 20-21
Plastic 4, 11, 14, 15, 18, 21, 22-23
Property 2, 6, 11
Rust 2, 20-21
Shatter 2, 8, 14-15
Soft 2, 6-7, 21
Springy 10-11
Steel 11, 20-21
Stretch 2, 8, 11, 12, 20
Strong 2, 8-9, 20
Tear 2, 8
Transparent 2, 15, 23
Water-resistant 19
Waterproof 2, 18, 19, 23
Weak 2, 8-9, 15

Science@School

Science@School is a series published by Atlantic Europe Publishing Company Ltd.

Atlantic Europe Publishing

Teacher's Guide
There is a Teacher's Guide to accompany this book, available only from the publisher.

CD-ROMs
There are CD-ROMs containing information to support the series. They are available from the publisher.

Dedicated Web Site
There's more information about other great Science@School packs and a wealth of supporting material available at our dedicated web site:

www.science-at-school.com

First published in 2001 by
Atlantic Europe Publishing Company Ltd

Copyright © 2001
Atlantic Europe Publishing Company Ltd

All rights reserved. No part of this publication may be reproduced, stored in a retrieval system, or transmitted in any form or by any means, electronic, mechanical, photocopying, recording or otherwise, without prior permission of the publisher.

Author
Brian Knapp, BSc, PhD

Educational Consultant
Peter Riley, BSc

Art Director
Duncan McCrae, BSc

Senior Designer
Adele Humphries, BA, PGCE

Editor
Lisa Magloff, BA

Illustrations
David Woodroffe

Designed and produced by
Earthscape Editions

Reproduced in Malaysia by
Global Colour

Printed in Hong Kong by
Wing King Tong Company Ltd

Suggested cataloguing location
Knapp, Brian
  Properties of materials – Science@School
  1. Materials – Juvenile Literature
  I. Title. II. Series
620.11

Paperback ISBN 1 86214 108 8
Hardback ISBN 1 86214 109 6

Picture credits
All photographs are from the Earthscape Editions photolibrary, except the following: (c=centre t=top b=bottom l=left r=right)
NASA 5b, 8bl.

This product is manufactured from sustainable managed forests. For every tree cut down at least one more is planted.